The Life Cycle of a

monarch
butterfly

by Julian May
photographs by Allan Roberts
A CREATIVE EDUCATION MINI BOOK

Distributed Exclusively by
CHILDRENS PRESS, CHICAGO

ISBN: 0-87191-240-6
Library of Congress Catalog Card Number: 73-1063

Contents

the
life cycle
of a
monarch
butterfly

milkweed butterfly

On bright summer days, many kinds of butterflies flutter over the flowers. They land, then uncoil a long tongue like a tiny drinking straw. The tongue thrusts deep into a flower, seeking a sweet juice called nectar.

If we tasted nectar, it would seem less sweet than plain water. But it has enough sugar to nourish insects such as this monarch butterfly.

The monarch, also called the milkweed butterfly, goes from flower to flower drinking nectar. Yellow flower dust called pollen sticks to it and is carried from one flower to the next.

By transferring pollen, the butterfly enables the flower to make seeds and reproduce itself. But the butterfly knows nothing of the useful work it does.

the egg

One sunny day, a female monarch will meet her mate. He transfers male cells to her body to fertilize tiny female cells that are waiting. This fertilization is something like the transfer of pollen in plants. In both cases, a male cell joins with a female cell to make a single new cell. This will grow into a new living thing just like the parents.

The union of male and female cells produces an egg. About the size of a pinhead, it is shiny and white with little ribs on the sides. A kind of glue from the mother monarch's body makes it stick tightly to the leaf she lays it on. No rain or wind can make it fall off.

Almost always, the mother monarch lays her eggs on milkweed. It will be the food-plant for her young.

the larva

Inside the egg, the original male and female cells have multiplied into millions. They gather together and make a tiny body—a very small caterpillar, or larva.

The newly hatched monarch larva is about one-sixteenth of an inch long, white with a dark head. It eats the egg-shell that sheltered it for three days. Then it starts to eat the milkweed leaf.

For about two weeks, the monarch larva eats and grows. Its skin does not stretch enough to hold its growing body, so it must molt, or shed the old skin, and grow a new one. The monarch larva molts five times, eating its old skin afterwards. Each time it molts, it grows larger.

When full grown, the larva is about two inches long. It has managed to escape many kinds of enemies.

The monarch caterpillar is striped with black, white, and yellow. Its head has several very tiny eyes and strong jaws to bite and chew leaves.

At the front and rear of its body are long "horns" that seem to be decorations. It has six true legs at the front of its body and eight "false" legs behind. It breathes through tiny holes in its sides.

When full grown, the larva undergoes a great change.

the chrysalis

The larva spins a tiny button of white silk and clings to it. Its skin splits up the back and slides upward.

With its new body, the insect clings briefly to the shed skin, then pokes tiny hooks into the silk button and lets the cast-off larval skin fall away.

Its new body is called a pupa or chrysalis (KRISS-uh-liss). It is a hard case, without legs.

When it is fresh, the chrysalis is rather long. Later, it will shrink and turn to a pale green color, decorated with golden knobs. Its outside is hard, like plastic, to protect the insect that is changing inside.

The change, called metamorphosis (MET-uh-MORE-fo-sis), transforms the chrysalis contents into a butterfly. The metamorphosis of the monarch takes about two weeks.

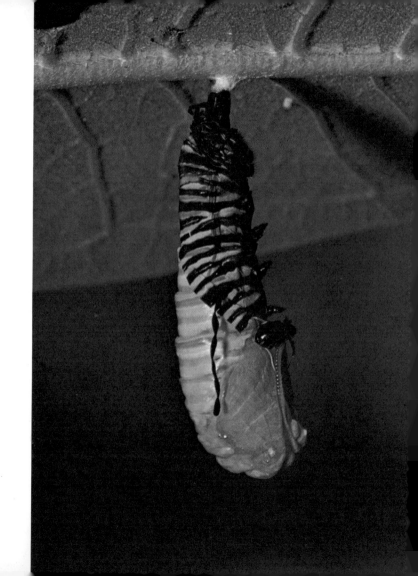

The last molt

The chrysalis

Cells that once formed the body of a wormlike larva now rearrange themselves. The caterpillar head, with its leaf-cutting jaws, disappears. A butterfly head with large eyes and a sucking tongue forms. The larva's long gut, which once digested green food, changes into a smaller stomach that will digest flower nectar. Long legs grow, and wings.

Finally the butterfly body is fully formed. The pale green chrysalis becomes transparent. It is time for the butterfly to come out.

The side of the case splits open. Out crawls a strange-looking creature with a fat abdomen and wadded-up wings of orange and black. It glistens with moisture and rests from the hard work of breaking out of the chrysalis.

the adult

Body fluid from the abdomen is pumped into the wings. They expand, while the abdomen shrinks and becomes slender. The butterfly must sit quietly for several hours while its wings dry and harden.

The insect in the picture is a male. We can tell by the oval scent gland on his wing. Scent helps him find a mate.

The butterfly waves his wings slowly, then faster and faster. Finally he takes off into the air. He flies without needing any lessons, folding his legs neatly.

Monarchs have light bodies and large wings. They are strong fliers and can travel great distances. They fly only in the daytime and are most active when the sun is out. When it rains, they hide under leaves.

The adult monarch's wings are covered with tiny colored scales. Under a microscope, they look like shingles on a roof. The upper side of the wings is orange-brown with black veins and a black edge spotted with white. The under side of the wings is pale orange. Two thread-like antennae crown the monarch's head. They are the butterfly's organs of smell.

migration

Each fall, adult monarchs migrate, or travel southward. Often they go in large swarms. They seem to start when the days shorten to a certain length. The butterflies do not have to think about their route. They have a built-in "sun compass" that takes them south.

They fly about 10 to 12 miles an hour. At night, they rest in trees.

Across fields, through cities, even over the Great Lakes the monarchs fly. Sometimes strong winds blow them into the water, but they are often able to take off again. They may fly 2,000 miles. When they reach warm, southern lands, they lay eggs. Their young will fly north again in spring, a few at a time, and be the parents of a new generation of northern monarchs the next year.

survival

Perhaps because they feed on bitter milkweed, monarchs seem to taste bad to birds. Not many of the large, colorful butterflies are eaten. For this reason, they are common over southern Canada, the United States except Alaska, and Mexico.

They have even spread to Asia and Europe with man's help, hitchhiking on ships.

RANGE OF MONARCH BUTTERFLY

Quite another kind of butterfly, the viceroy, has taken advantage of the monarch's survival ability. The viceroy looks just like a small monarch—except for a narrow black band across its lower wings.

If only the birds cared to taste the viceroy, they would find it delicious. But the insect's false colors save it. Disguised as a bad-tasting monarch, it lives in peace.

Other Creative Mini Books

Life Cycles

Life Cycle of a Bullfrog
Life Cycle of a Raccoon
Life Cycle of an Opossum
Life Cycle of a Moth
Life Cycle of a Rabbit
Life Cycle of a Fox
Life Cycle of a Turtle
Life Cycle of a Butterfly

World We Know

Fishes We Know
Birds We Know
Reptiles We Know
Mammals We Know
Insects We Know